"Keep your thoughts positive
Because your thoughts become
YOUR WORDS.

Keep your words positive
Because your words become
YOUR BEHAVIOR.

Keep your behavior positive
Because your behavior becomes
YOUR HABITS.

Keep your habits positive
Because your habits become
YOUR VALUES.

Keep your values positive
Because your values become
YOUR DESTINY."
-Mahatma Gandhi

About the Author

Angelica Alam is a financial services professional with over five years of experience in Treasury Services at various blue chip banking institutions on Wall Street. Prior to joining the financial sector, Angelica held strategy, operations, sales, marketing and business development roles in the media and entertainment industry with roles at major national broadcasters, including VH1 Classic and MTV Networks.

Aside from her professional accomplishments, Angelica is passionate about youth education and women's equality. Among her many community efforts, Angelica has served as a mentor for young women, providing support and guidance on their academic and educational goals and helping them to find scholarship opportunities and gain admission to some of the country's top colleges and universities. Angelica is also a part of numerous non-profit organizations focused on the advancement of inner city youth and is a recognized motivational speaker.

Angelica's biggest passion is the Let Me Be Great Foundation, an organization she founded in 2016 with a mission to connect youth with high quality and engaged mentors that will help them identify, plan for and achieve their short and long term academic and professional goals.

Angelica earned a Bachelor of Arts in Economics from the University of California at Riverside and a Master of Business Administration from the Darden School of Business at the University of Virginia.

"My goal is that this journal allows you to get one step closer to discovering your purpose. Treat this journal as if you are writing the story of your future. You are the author of your destiny. May this journal serve as a motivator as you pursue all of your goals. Dismiss all limiting beliefs and self doubt; be fearless and confident in all that you pursue"

– Angelica Alam

Introduction

Often times we begin goal planning by thinking of these big, fancy milestone goals that get us excited. We want to start a business or we want to lose weight or we want to travel the world or if you are anything like me you want to do all three and conquer the universe - at the same time! There is nothing wrong with being ambitious. Milestone goals are great and having many is healthy and encouraged. With that being said, the more goals you have the more important it is to be organized and calculated. I used to overwhelm myself constantly when I would goal plan because I would have big goals but failed to organize my thoughts and to track my small wins. Hence why I created this simple journal, so that we can break down our big goals into small action items that can easily be tracked and tackled one by one.

Some words of advice as you work through planning your goals:

1. Break down your big goals into individual small goals. For example, if you want to start a business, think of all the small steps that need to be taken to start a business and treat each step as an individual goal.

2. Be concise – I kept the lines short on purpose. Be clear and to the point with your goals and action items. Do not overwhelm yourself by being long-winded. Stick to the point, keep it short, and keep it direct.

3. I added 2 reference pages at the end of the journal so that you can keep track of each goal, the page number, and the date you created it. Revisit each goal as needed. These reference pages were added so that you can keep your goals organized and easy to revisit.

4. Do not over complicate the resource and action planning section. Organize your thoughts and use your resources wisely.

5. Personal reflection is important. Be honest but kind to yourself. If your goals do not push you to become a stronger, smarter, better version of you then you must revisit these goals and revise as needed.

6. The quotes in between are meant to be a combination of motivational quotes and self-declarations. Use them as needed and feel free to use those pages to reflect on how the quotes make you feel.

7. Most importantly, get comfortable with declaring greatness and positivity over your life. The positive affirmations are so that you can get comfortable with owning your greatness. The declarations in between the goals serve as a motivator for you to embrace your strength and purpose!

Dedicated to:

The greatness in you.

Our youth and their success.

My beautiful family.

May you always remember to be:

CONFIDENT

Self-confidence is the foundation of all great success and achievement.

RESILIENT

Embrace the unknown and be fearless in all that you pursue.

UNSTOPPABLE

Be bold, be daring, and get comfortable with being uncomfortable.

My goal for this journal is:

_____

_____

_____

_____

_____

_____

_____

_____

_____

_____

Today's Date: _____

Today I make the commitment to dedicate time and positive energy to
creating the future of which I have always dreamed.

- GOAL -

_____

_____

- RESOURCES NEEDED -

1. _____

2. _____

3. _____

4. _____

5. _____

- ACTION PLAN -

1. _____

2. _____

3. _____

4. _____

5. _____

- POSITIVE AFFIRMATIONS -

1. _____

2. _____

3. _____

4. _____

5. _____

I CAN
AND
I WILL.

It is not about pursuing perfection.
It is about applying consistent effort.
When you bring effort every single day,
That's when transformation begins to happen.
That's how change occurs.
Do not be afraid of change.
Be afraid of staying in the same place.

I am going to make myself very proud one day.

I BELIEVE in all of my greatness.

I DISMISS all limiting beliefs.

I EMBRACE the power to create change.

- GOAL -

_____

_____

- RESOURCES NEEDED -

1. _____

2. _____

3. _____

4. _____

5. _____

- ACTION PLAN -

1. _____

2. _____

3. _____

4. _____

5. _____

- POSITIVE AFFIRMATIONS -

1. _____

2. _____

3. _____

4. _____

5. _____

I am going to make myself very proud one day.

I BELIEVE in all of my greatness.

I DISMISS all limiting beliefs.

I EMBRACE the power to create change.

- GOAL -

_____

_____

- RESOURCES NEEDED -

1. _____

2. _____

3. _____

4. _____

5. _____

- ACTION PLAN -

1. _____

2. _____

3. _____

4. _____

5. _____

- POSITIVE AFFIRMATIONS -

1. _____

2. _____

3. _____

4. _____

5. _____

DREAM
BIG.
WORK
SMART.

I am a powerful person.
I am in control of myself.
I am the author of my destiny.

I will face whatever comes today with a positive attitude.
Even in the face of adversity,
I will be STRONG and FAITHFUL.

- GOAL -

_____

_____

- RESOURCES NEEDED -

1. _____

2. _____

3. _____

4. _____

5. _____

- ACTION PLAN -

1. _____

2. _____

3. _____

4. _____

5. _____

- POSITIVE AFFIRMATIONS -

1. _____

2. _____

3. _____

4. _____

5. _____

BELIEVE
AND
TRUST
IN YOU.

I can. I will. I must.

This is my time to shine.

- GOAL -

_____

_____

- RESOURCES NEEDED -

1. _____

2. _____

3. _____

4. _____

5. _____

- ACTION PLAN -

1. _____

2. _____

3. _____

4. _____

5. _____

- POSITIVE AFFIRMATIONS -

1. _____

2. _____

3. _____

4. _____

5. _____

I
BELIEVE
IN
MYSELF.

Nothing will hold me back.

I get closer to my dreams with each passing day.

- GOAL -

_____

_____

- RESOURCES NEEDED -

1. _____

2. _____

3. _____

4. _____

5. _____

- ACTION PLAN -

1. _____

2. _____

3. _____

4. _____

5. _____

- POSITIVE AFFIRMATIONS -

1. _____

2. _____

3. _____

4. _____

5. _____

I
WILL
ALWAYS
WIN.

I will not keep watching the clock
I will do what it does and
KEEP GOING.

I am so much STRONGER than I think and
I will prove it to myself by not giving up.

- GOAL -

_____

_____

- RESOURCES NEEDED -

1. _____

2. _____

3. _____

4. _____

5. _____

- ACTION PLAN -

1. _____

2. _____

3. _____

4. _____

5. _____

- POSITIVE AFFIRMATIONS -

1. _____

2. _____

3. _____

4. _____

5. _____

I AM
SO
PROUD
OF ME.

I choose
success,
happiness,
and abundance in my life!

I am never losing.
I am always learning and growing.

- GOAL -

_____

_____

- RESOURCES NEEDED -

1. _____

2. _____

3. _____

4. _____

5. _____

- ACTION PLAN -

1. _____

2. _____

3. _____

4. _____

5. _____

- POSITIVE AFFIRMATIONS -

1. _____

2. _____

3. _____

4. _____

5. _____

I AM
READY
TO BE
GREAT.

Success is a series of small wins.
I will celebrate all of my wins.

I release fear, doubt and worry.

- GOAL -

_____

_____

- RESOURCES NEEDED -

1. _____

2. _____

3. _____

4. _____

5. _____

- ACTION PLAN -

1. _____

2. _____

3. _____

4. _____

5. _____

- POSITIVE AFFIRMATIONS -

1. _____

2. _____

3. _____

4. _____

5. _____

I
TRUST
IN
MYSELF.

My potential to succeed is infinite.

I excel in all that I do.

- GOAL -

_____

_____

- RESOURCES NEEDED -

1. _____

2. _____

3. _____

4. _____

5. _____

- ACTION PLAN -

1. _____

2. _____

3. _____

4. _____

5. _____

- POSITIVE AFFIRMATIONS -

1. _____

2. _____

3. _____

4. _____

5. _____

I
CLAIM
VICTORY
NOW.

I will win, not immediately, but DEFINITELY.

I aspire to INSPIRE.

- GOAL -

_____

_____

- RESOURCES NEEDED -

1. _____

2. _____

3. _____

4. _____

5. _____

- ACTION PLAN -

1. _____

2. _____

3. _____

4. _____

5. _____

- POSITIVE AFFIRMATIONS -

1. _____

2. _____

3. _____

4. _____

5. _____

I
DARE
TO
DREAM.

I will TRUST the wait.
I will EMBRACE the uncertainty.
I will ENJOY the beauty of becoming.
When nothing is certain,
I KNOW THAT ANYTHING IS POSSIBLE.

Only I can change my life, no one can do it for me.

- GOAL -

_____

_____

- RESOURCES NEEDED -

1. _____

2. _____

3. _____

4. _____

5. _____

- ACTION PLAN -

1. _____

2. _____

3. _____

4. _____

5. _____

- POSITIVE AFFIRMATIONS -

1. _____

2. _____

3. _____

4. _____

5. _____

- PERSONAL REFLECTION -

I AM
READY
TO
INSPIRE.

A negative mind will never give me a positive life.

It always seems impossible until it is done.
So I CAN, MUST and WILL DO IT.

- GOAL -

_____

_____

- RESOURCES NEEDED -

1. _____

2. _____

3. _____

4. _____

5. _____

- ACTION PLAN -

1. _____

2. _____

3. _____

4. _____

5. _____

- POSITIVE AFFIRMATIONS -

1. _____

2. _____

3. _____

4. _____

5. _____

I
AM
NOT
AFRAID.

The expert in anything was once a beginner.

With every lesson, I will continue to build my skill sets.

I will seek opportunities of growth.

I will challenge myself in healthy ways that will help me evolve.

There is no substitution for hard work.

I will work HARD.

I will push all of my limits.

I will AIM HIGHER.

- GOAL -

_____

_____

- RESOURCES NEEDED -

1. _____

2. _____

3. _____

4. _____

5. _____

- ACTION PLAN -

1. _____

2. _____

3. _____

4. _____

5. _____

- POSITIVE AFFIRMATIONS -

1. _____

2. _____

3. _____

4. _____

5. _____

I AM
STRONG
AND
READY.

Courage does not mean I am not afraid.
It means I will not let my fear stop me.
I will be FEARLESS in all that I do.

I will never let my emotions overpower my intelligence.
I will build emotional strength.
I believe in the power of mind over matter.

- GOAL -

_____

_____

- RESOURCES NEEDED -

1. _____

2. _____

3. _____

4. _____

5. _____

- ACTION PLAN -

1. _____

2. _____

3. _____

4. _____

5. _____

- POSITIVE AFFIRMATIONS -

1. _____

2. _____

3. _____

4. _____

5. _____

I will never let my emotions overpower my intelligence.

I will build emotional strength.

I believe in the power of mind over matter.

- GOAL -

_____

_____

- RESOURCES NEEDED -

1. _____

2. _____

3. _____

4. _____

5. _____

- ACTION PLAN -

1. _____

2. _____

3. _____

4. _____

5. _____

- POSITIVE AFFIRMATIONS -

1. _____

2. _____

3. _____

4. _____

5. _____

I
HAVE
FAITH
IN ME.

I will not wait for opportunities,
I will CREATE them.

I understand that winners are not people who never fail;
They are people who NEVER QUIT.
I will NEVER QUIT.

- GOAL -

_____

_____

- RESOURCES NEEDED -

1. _____

2. _____

3. _____

4. _____

5. _____

- ACTION PLAN -

1. _____

2. _____

3. _____

4. _____

5. _____

- POSITIVE AFFIRMATIONS -

1. _____

2. _____

3. _____

4. _____

5. _____

I AM
WISE,
FREE &
GIFTED.

I did not wake up today to be mediocre.
I wake up everyday knowing that I am GREAT.
I own my greatness and exercise it daily.

I will stay positive, work hard, and make it happen.
Even when I am weary – I will forge ahead.

- GOAL -

_____

_____

- RESOURCES NEEDED -

1. _____

2. _____

3. _____

4. _____

5. _____

- ACTION PLAN -

1. _____

2. _____

3. _____

4. _____

5. _____

- POSITIVE AFFIRMATIONS -

1. _____

2. _____

3. _____

4. _____

5. _____

I AM
LOYAL
TO MY
FAITH.

I will stop saying, "I wish" and start declaring, "I will!"
I declare that I will put actions behind my faith.
I will take bold steps to move in the direction
of my passion and purpose.

I know that success occurs when
opportunity meets preparation.
I will be prepared for every opportunity that comes my way.

- GOAL -

_____

_____

- RESOURCES NEEDED -

1. _____

2. _____

3. _____

4. _____

5. _____

- ACTION PLAN -

1. _____

2. _____

3. _____

4. _____

5. _____

- POSITIVE AFFIRMATIONS -

1. _____

2. _____

3. _____

4. _____

5. _____

I AM
ALWAYS
A
WINNER.

I will focus all of my energy NOT on fighting the old,
but on BUILDING the NEW.

Most great people have attained their greatest success
just one step beyond their greatest failure.
I will treat my failures as a sign of redirection.
I will not accept rejection.
I will allow all of my mishaps to guide me to my true path.

- GOAL -

_____

_____

- RESOURCES NEEDED -

1. _____

2. _____

3. _____

4. _____

5. _____

- ACTION PLAN -

1. _____

2. _____

3. _____

4. _____

5. _____

- POSITIVE AFFIRMATIONS -

1. _____

2. _____

3. _____

4. _____

5. _____

I AM
WISE
AND
STRONG.

I never lose.
Either I WIN
Or I LEARN.

I will NEVER give up.
I will stay FOCUSED.
I will stay POSITIVE.
I will stay STRONG.

- GOAL -

_____

_____

- RESOURCES NEEDED -

1. _____

2. _____

3. _____

4. _____

5. _____

- ACTION PLAN -

1. _____

2. _____

3. _____

4. _____

5. _____

- POSITIVE AFFIRMATIONS -

1. _____

2. _____

3. _____

4. _____

5. _____

I AM
ABLE
AND
WORTHY.

I am ready because I know that
every next level of my life will demand
a different, better, and stronger
version of myself.

I am ready, willing, and able to be that
different, better and stronger
version of myself.

I know that EXCELLENCE is my journey and
DISCIPLINE will be my vehicle!

- GOAL -

_____

_____

- RESOURCES NEEDED -

1. _____

2. _____

3. _____

4. _____

5. _____

- ACTION PLAN -

1. _____

2. _____

3. _____

4. _____

5. _____

- POSITIVE AFFIRMATIONS -

1. _____

2. _____

3. _____

4. _____

5. _____

I know that EXCELLENCE is my journey and
DISCIPLINE will be my vehicle!

- GOAL -

_____

_____

- RESOURCES NEEDED -

1. _____

2. _____

3. _____

4. _____

5. _____

- ACTION PLAN -

1. _____

2. _____

3. _____

4. _____

5. _____

- POSITIVE AFFIRMATIONS -

1. _____

2. _____

3. _____

4. _____

5. _____

I
ASPIRE
TO
INSPIRE.

Motivation gets me going but
DISCIPLINE keeps me growing.
I will stay motivated and disciplined.

Life is 10% what happens to me and 90% how I react to it.
I will think before I speak.
I will be in control of my reactions.
I will let go of the things I cannot control.

- GOAL -

_____

_____

- RESOURCES NEEDED -

1. _____

2. _____

3. _____

4. _____

5. _____

- ACTION PLAN -

1. _____

2. _____

3. _____

4. _____

5. _____

- POSITIVE AFFIRMATIONS -

1. _____

2. _____

3. _____

4. _____

5. _____

- PERSONAL REFLECTION -

TOUGH
TIMES
NEVER
LAST.

7

I will make my life a masterpiece;
I will have no limitations
on what I can have, be, or do.

I trust in my genius.

I know more than I think I do.

- GOAL -

_____

_____

- RESOURCES NEEDED -

I. _____

2. _____

3. _____

4. _____

5. _____

- ACTION PLAN -

I. _____

2. _____

3. _____

4. _____

5. _____

- POSITIVE AFFIRMATIONS -

I. _____

2. _____

3. _____

4. _____

5. _____

PUSH HARDER, BELIEVE BIGGER.

Sometimes I am tested not to show my weaknesses,
but to discover my strengths.
I am excited to discover all of my strengths.
I will PASS all of the tests life brings my way.

I know that it will not be easy,
but it will absolutely be worth it!

- GOAL -

_____

_____

- RESOURCES NEEDED -

1. _____

2. _____

3. _____

4. _____

5. _____

- ACTION PLAN -

1. _____

2. _____

3. _____

4. _____

5. _____

- POSITIVE AFFIRMATIONS -

1. _____

2. _____

3. _____

4. _____

5. _____

I know that it will not be easy,
but it will absolutely be worth it!

- GOAL -

_____

_____

- RESOURCES NEEDED -

1. _____

2. _____

3. _____

4. _____

5. _____

- ACTION PLAN -

1. _____

2. _____

3. _____

4. _____

5. _____

- POSITIVE AFFIRMATIONS -

1. _____

2. _____

3. _____

4. _____

5. _____

I
TRUST
IN MY
GIFTS.

Excuses will not get me results.
Creating a plan, executing that plan and working hard
will get me the results I need to be successful.

I will not downgrade my dream to fit my reality.
I will upgrade my conviction to match my destiny.

I DARE TO DREAM!

- GOAL -

_____

_____

- RESOURCES NEEDED -

1. _____

2. _____

3. _____

4. _____

5. _____

- ACTION PLAN -

1. _____

2. _____

3. _____

4. _____

5. _____

- POSITIVE AFFIRMATIONS -

1. _____

2. _____

3. _____

4. _____

5. _____

I AM
TRUE TO
BEING
MYSELF.

I declare I will not just survive.

I will not just exist.

I will live an abundant life.

I will thrive.

I will prosper despite any difficulty that may come my way.

I declare I am EXTRAORDINARY.
There is no one like me and that is my POWER.

- GOAL -

_____

_____

- RESOURCES NEEDED -

1. _____

2. _____

3. _____

4. _____

5. _____

- ACTION PLAN -

1. _____

2. _____

3. _____

4. _____

5. _____

- POSITIVE AFFIRMATIONS -

1. _____

2. _____

3. _____

4. _____

5. _____

ASPIRE
TO
BE
GREAT.

I AM A SURVIVOR.

I will commit to my SUCCESS.

I will NOT believe anyone when they say I cannot do it.

A negative mind will never bring me a positive life.
I will shift to dominant thoughts and feelings of love and gratitude.

- GOAL -

_____

_____

- RESOURCES NEEDED -

1. _____

2. _____

3. _____

4. _____

5. _____

- ACTION PLAN -

1. _____

2. _____

3. _____

4. _____

5. _____

- POSITIVE AFFIRMATIONS -

1. _____

2. _____

3. _____

4. _____

5. _____

I CAN
AND
I WILL.

My goals will be so strong
That obstacles, failure and loss
will only act as motivation.

I will put my heart, mind, intellect, and soul
even to my smallest acts.

- GOAL -

_____

_____

- RESOURCES NEEDED -

1. _____

2. _____

3. _____

4. _____

5. _____

- ACTION PLAN -

1. _____

2. _____

3. _____

4. _____

5. _____

- POSITIVE AFFIRMATIONS -

1. _____

2. _____

3. _____

4. _____

5. _____

DREAM
BIG,
WORK
SMART.

I know what I want and
I AM GOING TO GET IT.

I may not be there yet,
but I am closer than I was yesterday.

- GOAL -

_____

_____

- RESOURCES NEEDED -

1. _____

2. _____

3. _____

4. _____

5. _____

- ACTION PLAN -

1. _____

2. _____

3. _____

4. _____

5. _____

- POSITIVE AFFIRMATIONS -

1. _____

2. _____

3. _____

4. _____

5. _____

BELIEVE
AND
TRUST
IN YOU.

It is my determination and persistence that will make me a successful person.

I am not what has happened to me.
I am what I choose to become.
I choose to be a winner.

- GOAL -

_____

_____

- RESOURCES NEEDED -

1. _____

2. _____

3. _____

4. _____

5. _____

- ACTION PLAN -

1. _____

2. _____

3. _____

4. _____

5. _____

- POSITIVE AFFIRMATIONS -

1. _____

2. _____

3. _____

4. _____

5. _____

I
BELIEVE
IN
MYSELF.

When I look in the mirror,
I realize that is my only competition.

Hard work beats talent,
when talent doesn't work hard.
My work ethic is fierce.

- GOAL -

_____

_____

- RESOURCES NEEDED -

1. _____

2. _____

3. _____

4. _____

5. _____

- ACTION PLAN -

1. _____

2. _____

3. _____

4. _____

5. _____

- POSITIVE AFFIRMATIONS -

1. _____

2. _____

3. _____

4. _____

5. _____

I
WILL
ALWAYS
WIN.

I am replacing excuses with effort.
I am replacing laziness with determination.

I know my limitations and
I am ready to defy them.

- GOAL -

_____

_____

- RESOURCES NEEDED -

1. _____

2. _____

3. _____

4. _____

5. _____

- ACTION PLAN -

1. _____

2. _____

3. _____

4. _____

5. _____

- POSITIVE AFFIRMATIONS -

1. _____

2. _____

3. _____

4. _____

5. _____

I AM
SO
PROUD
OF ME.

My mission is to be so busy building
the life I have always dreamed of,
that I have no time for
hate, regret, worry or fear.

Let me be great, because my desire to succeed
is stronger than my fears.

- GOAL -

_____

_____

- RESOURCES NEEDED -

1. _____

2. _____

3. _____

4. _____

5. _____

- ACTION PLAN -

1. _____

2. _____

3. _____

4. _____

5. _____

- POSITIVE AFFIRMATIONS -

1. _____

2. _____

3. _____

4. _____

5. _____

I AM
READY
TO BE
GREAT.

Developing a strong mindset
is one of my daily habits.
Everyday I get stronger.

Believing in myself is one of my strongest beliefs.

- GOAL -

_____

_____

- RESOURCES NEEDED -

1. _____

2. _____

3. _____

4. _____

5. _____

- ACTION PLAN -

1. _____

2. _____

3. _____

4. _____

5. _____

- POSITIVE AFFIRMATIONS -

1. _____

2. _____

3. _____

4. _____

5. _____

I
TRUST
IN
MYSELF.

My optimism today,
will determine my level of success tomorrow.

I will not waste a good mistake.

I will learn from it.

- GOAL -

_____

_____

- RESOURCES NEEDED -

1. _____

2. _____

3. _____

4. _____

5. _____

- ACTION PLAN -

1. _____

2. _____

3. _____

4. _____

5. _____

- POSITIVE AFFIRMATIONS -

1. _____

2. _____

3. _____

4. _____

5. _____

I
CLAIM
VICTORY
NOW.

Everyday is a new beginning.
Take a deep breath and start again.

I am capable.
I am strong.
I believe in myself,
I will turn my dreams into a plan.
I will turn my plan into my reality.

- GOAL -

_____

_____

- RESOURCES NEEDED -

I. _____

2. _____

3. _____

4. _____

5. _____

- ACTION PLAN -

I. _____

2. _____

3. _____

4. _____

5. _____

- POSITIVE AFFIRMATIONS -

I. _____

2. _____

3. _____

4. _____

5. _____

I
DARE
TO
DREAM.

I am thankful for all of those who said no to me.
It is because of them that I am doing it myself.

I want to inspire people.

I want someone to look at me and say,

"because of you, I did not give up"

- GOAL -

_____

_____

- RESOURCES NEEDED -

1. _____

2. _____

3. _____

4. _____

5. _____

- ACTION PLAN -

1. _____

2. _____

3. _____

4. _____

5. _____

- POSITIVE AFFIRMATIONS -

1. _____

2. _____

3. _____

4. _____

5. _____

_____

_____

_____

_____

_____

_____

_____

_____

_____

_____

_____

_____

I AM READY TO INSPIRE.

Worrying does not take away tomorrow's trouble,
it takes away today's peace.
I am done worrying.

I will stop focusing on how stressed I am.
I will instead focus on how blessed I am.

- GOAL -

_____

_____

- RESOURCES NEEDED -

1. _____

2. _____

3. _____

4. _____

5. _____

- ACTION PLAN -

1. _____

2. _____

3. _____

4. _____

5. _____

- POSITIVE AFFIRMATIONS -

1. _____

2. _____

3. _____

4. _____

5. _____

I
AM
NOT
AFRAID.

I have been assigned this mountain
to show others that it can be moved.

Knowing myself is
the beginning of all wisdom.

- GOAL -

_____

_____

- RESOURCES NEEDED -

1. _____

2. _____

3. _____

4. _____

5. _____

- ACTION PLAN -

1. _____

2. _____

3. _____

4. _____

5. _____

- POSITIVE AFFIRMATIONS -

1. _____

2. _____

3. _____

4. _____

5. _____

I AM
STRONG
AND
READY.

Be a gentle with yourself,
you are doing the best you can.

You can be the most perfect peace in the bunch
and there will always be someone who
does not like peaches.

Stop worrying about what others think
and do what makes you happy.

- GOAL -

_____

_____

- RESOURCES NEEDED -

1. _____

2. _____

3. _____

4. _____

5. _____

- ACTION PLAN -

1. _____

2. _____

3. _____

4. _____

5. _____

- POSITIVE AFFIRMATIONS -

1. _____

2. _____

3. _____

4. _____

5. _____

I
HAVE
FAITH
IN ME.

Whatever you decide to do,
make sure it makes you happy.

Practice like you never won.
Perform like you never lost.

- GOAL -

_____

_____

- RESOURCES NEEDED -

1. _____

2. _____

3. _____

4. _____

5. _____

- ACTION PLAN -

1. _____

2. _____

3. _____

4. _____

5. _____

- POSITIVE AFFIRMATIONS -

1. _____

2. _____

3. _____

4. _____

5. _____

I AM
WISE,
FREE &
GIFTED

Just because my path is different,
It does not mean I am lost.

My best teacher is my last mistake.

- GOAL -

_____

_____

- RESOURCES NEEDED -

1. _____

2. _____

3. _____

4. _____

5. _____

- ACTION PLAN -

1. _____

2. _____

3. _____

4. _____

5. _____

- POSITIVE AFFIRMATIONS -

1. _____

2. _____

3. _____

4. _____

5. _____

My best teacher is my last mistake.

- GOAL -

_____

_____

- RESOURCES NEEDED -

1. _____

2. _____

3. _____

4. _____

5. _____

- ACTION PLAN -

1. _____

2. _____

3. _____

4. _____

5. _____

- POSITIVE AFFIRMATIONS -

1. _____

2. _____

3. _____

4. _____

5. _____

I AM
LOYAL
TO MY
FAITH.

It is never too late for me
to be who I might have been.

Success is not a one-time thing.
It is a habit and a way of life.

- GOAL -

_____

_____

- RESOURCES NEEDED -

1. _____

2. _____

3. _____

4. _____

5. _____

- ACTION PLAN -

1. _____

2. _____

3. _____

4. _____

5. _____

- POSITIVE AFFIRMATIONS -

1. _____

2. _____

3. _____

4. _____

5. _____

I AM
ALWAYS
A
WINNER.

My intuition is always on my side.

Do not lose your present to your past.

Let it GO.

- GOAL -

_____

_____

- RESOURCES NEEDED -

1. _____

2. _____

3. _____

4. _____

5. _____

- ACTION PLAN -

1. _____

2. _____

3. _____

4. _____

5. _____

- POSITIVE AFFIRMATIONS -

1. _____

2. _____

3. _____

4. _____

5. _____

I AM
WISE
AND
STRONG.

I will prove them all wrong.

Let your sense of purpose lead the way.

- GOAL -

_____

_____

- RESOURCES NEEDED -

1. _____

2. _____

3. _____

4. _____

5. _____

- ACTION PLAN -

1. _____

2. _____

3. _____

4. _____

5. _____

- POSITIVE AFFIRMATIONS -

1. _____

2. _____

3. _____

4. _____

5. _____

Let your sense of purpose lead the way.

- GOAL -

_____

_____

- RESOURCES NEEDED -

1. _____

2. _____

3. _____

4. _____

5. _____

- ACTION PLAN -

1. _____

2. _____

3. _____

4. _____

5. _____

- POSITIVE AFFIRMATIONS -

1. _____

2. _____

3. _____

4. _____

5. _____

I AM
ABLE
AND
WORTHY.

I am allowed to be both
a masterpiece and a work in progress,
simultaneously.

Take every chance you get in life,
because some things only happen once.

Live life to the fullest.
Do not take one moment for granted.

- GOAL -

_____

_____

- RESOURCES NEEDED -

1. _____

2. _____

3. _____

4. _____

5. _____

- ACTION PLAN -

1. _____

2. _____

3. _____

4. _____

5. _____

- POSITIVE AFFIRMATIONS -

1. _____

2. _____

3. _____

4. _____

5. _____

I
ASPIRE
TO
INSPIRE.

Great things never come from comfort zone.

Get up every morning
and remind yourself
"I CAN DO THIS".

- GOAL -

_____

_____

- RESOURCES NEEDED -

1. _____

2. _____

3. _____

4. _____

5. _____

- ACTION PLAN -

1. _____

2. _____

3. _____

4. _____

5. _____

- POSITIVE AFFIRMATIONS -

1. _____

2. _____

3. _____

4. _____

5. _____

TOUGH
TIMES
NEVER
LAST.

Doubt kills more dreams than failure.

My only limit is myself.
When I look in the mirror,
there exists my biggest competition.

Everyday I strive to be better
than the person I was yesterday.

- GOAL -

_____

_____

- RESOURCES NEEDED -

1. _____

2. _____

3. _____

4. _____

5. _____

- ACTION PLAN -

1. _____

2. _____

3. _____

4. _____

5. _____

- POSITIVE AFFIRMATIONS -

1. _____

2. _____

3. _____

4. _____

5. _____

PUSH
HARDER
BELIEVE
BIGGER.

I am done waiting for things to happen.
I am ready to go out and make things happen.

Even before I started,
I knew I would win.

- GOAL -

_____

_____

- RESOURCES NEEDED -

1. _____

2. _____

3. _____

4. _____

5. _____

- ACTION PLAN -

1. _____

2. _____

3. _____

4. _____

5. _____

- POSITIVE AFFIRMATIONS -

1. _____

2. _____

3. _____

4. _____

5. _____

I
TRUST
IN MY
GIFTS.

To succeed, I will believe in my abilities
with such a passion that it will become a reality!

- GOAL -

_____

_____

- RESOURCES NEEDED -

1. _____

2. _____

3. _____

4. _____

5. _____

- ACTION PLAN -

1. _____

2. _____

3. _____

4. _____

5. _____

- POSITIVE AFFIRMATIONS -

1. _____

2. _____

3. _____

4. _____

5. _____

- PERSONAL REFLECTION -

I AM
TRUE TO
BEING
MYSELF.

GOAL REFERENCE

Goal _____ Pg. ___ Date: _____

Goal _____ Pg. ___ Date: _____

Goal _____ Pg. ___ Date: _____

Goal _____ Pg. ___ Date: _____

Goal _____ Pg. ___ Date: _____

Goal _____ Pg. ___ Date: _____

Goal _____ Pg. ___ Date: _____

Goal _____ Pg. ___ Date: _____

Goal _____ Pg. ___ Date: _____

Goal _____ Pg. ___ Date: _____

Goal _____ Pg. ___ Date: _____

Goal _____ Pg. ___ Date: _____

Goal _____ Pg. ___ Date: _____

Goal _____ Pg. ___ Date: _____

Goal _____ Pg. ___ Date: _____

Goal _____ Pg. ___ Date: _____

Goal _____ Pg. ___ Date: _____

Goal _____ Pg. ___ Date: _____

Goal _____ Pg. ___ Date: _____

Goal _____ Pg. ___ Date: _____

Goal _____ Pg. ___ Date: _____

Goal _____ Pg. ___ Date: _____

Goal _____ Pg. ___ Date: _____

Goal _____ Pg. ___ Date: _____

Goal _____ Pg. ___ Date: _____

Goal _____ Pg. ___ Date: _____

Goal _____ Pg. ___ Date: _____

Goal _____ Pg. ___ Date: _____

Goal _____ Pg. ___ Date:

GOAL REFERENCE

Goal _____ Pg. ___ Date: _____

Goal _____ Pg. ___ Date: _____

Goal _____ Pg. ___ Date: _____

Goal _____ Pg. ___ Date: _____

Goal _____ Pg. ___ Date: _____

Goal _____ Pg. ___ Date: _____

Goal _____ Pg. ___ Date: _____

Goal _____ Pg. ___ Date: _____

Goal _____ Pg. ___ Date: _____

Goal _____ Pg. ___ Date: _____

Goal _____ Pg. ___ Date: _____

Goal _____ Pg. ___ Date: _____

Goal _____ Pg. ___ Date: _____

Goal _____ Pg. ___ Date: _____

Goal _____ Pg. ___ Date: _____

Goal _____ Pg. ___ Date: _____

Goal _____ Pg. ___ Date: _____

Goal _____ Pg. ___ Date: _____

Goal _____ Pg. ___ Date: _____

Goal _____ Pg. ___ Date: _____

Goal _____ Pg. ___ Date: _____

Goal _____ Pg. ___ Date: _____

Goal _____ Pg. ___ Date: _____

Goal _____ Pg. ___ Date: _____

Goal _____ Pg. ___ Date: _____

Goal _____ Pg. ___ Date: _____

Goal _____ Pg. ___ Date: _____

Goal _____ Pg. ___ Date: _____

Made in the USA
Middletown, DE
13 June 2020

9783425OR00113